# 100 Ways to Find Investment Ideas

---

THE INVESTORS' REFERENCE FOR
GENERATING ACTIONABLE
INVESTMENT OPPORTUNITIES

## Mariusz Skonieczny

Investment Publishing

Mariusz Skonieczny/Investment Publishing
1202 Far Pond Cir
Mishawaka, IN 46544
www.classicvalueinvestors.com

Ordering Information:
Quantity sales. Special discounts are available on quantity purchases by corporations, associations, and others. For details, contact the "Special Sales Department" at the address above.

100 Ways to Find Investment Ideas/ Mariusz Skonieczny. —1st ed.
ISBN 978-0-9848490-2-4

# Table of Contents

# Preface

All investors in the stock market face one common challenge—finding new investment ideas. While it may seem like there are a lot of companies to choose from, only a few will be true winners, and it can be difficult to identify them. There is no one right way to do it, and every investor does it a little differently, using different sources. There are many ways to find them. You can read blogs, listen to podcasts, perform keyword searches, or interview other investors.

In this book, I will show you 100 ways to generate actionable investment opportunities. If you are already an investor, you have probably used some of these sources but may have never heard of others. The idea is to expose you to various possibilities. Also, many of them can be used for due diligence.

Obviously, you don't have to use them all. I have a few methods that I prefer and they generate enough ideas to keep me busy. I hope that you will find this book useful and that it will help you reach your investment goals.

# Value Investors Club

Value Investors Club (Valueinvestorsclub.com) is an exclusive club that is popular among value investors. It was started by Joel Greenblatt and John Petry. Greenblatt is the author of three books: *You Can Be a Stock Market Genius*, *The Little Book that Beats the Market*, and *The Big Secret for the Small Investor*. He is a managing principal and co-chief investment officer of Gotham Asset Management. Petry is the founder and chief compliance officer of Sessa Capital.

Value Investors Club is a group that allows members to share value and special situation investment ideas with each other. The membership was originally capped at 250 members but there are now several hundred. However, they continue to be highly selective when granting membership. Twice a month, the club awards $5,000 for the best investment idea. To be accepted into the club, an individual must complete an application and submit an investment idea.

In order to keep the quality of ideas high, members are allowed to submit no more than six write-ups per year. The club wants only the best opportunities. Each member must submit a minimum of two investment ideas per year.

Investors who apply and are not accepted can still benefit from the site. Any investor can sign up by providing their e-mail address, and this allows them to see all the ideas with a 45-day delay. In value investing, this is usually not a problem because many value investing ideas take months and years to work out.

# SumZero

SumZero (Sumzero.com) is a website for professional investors who are part of the "buy side." It was started in April 2008 by Divya Narendra and Aalap Mahadevia who had a vision to change how professional investors shared information with each other. The site has more than 10,000 buy-side professionals who submit investment ideas in order to access other people's ideas. In order to join, each professional member has to meet the site's strict guidelines. The person has to work at the research department of a hedge fund, mutual fund, private equity fund, or investment bank. He or she must apply with an investment idea that will be evaluated by SumZero.

Even though individual investors are not allowed to join, they can still get investment ideas through a variety of free and premium offerings. They can register for basic membership which allows them to receive weekly and quarterly communications that include investment opportunities. SumZero has more than 40,000 basic members.

# Distressed Debt Investors Club

D istressed      Debt      Investors      Club (Distresseddebtinvestorsclub.com) was modeled after Value Investors Club meaning that it is an exclusive club that allows guest members to view ideas with a delay (50-day delay). The club was started in 2009 by an individual that goes by the name Hunter. He was a investment professional at a large money management firm focused on high yield and distressed debt investing.

Even though the name of the club includes the word "debt," investors can find plenty of equity investment opportunities which may be undervalued stocks or special situations. The membership is capped at 250 members who have to pay $49.95 per year to maintain access. To attract only the highest quality investors, members have to be approved through an application process which includes an idea submission. Similar to Value Investors Club, members of DDIC must submit two ideas per year. In addition, they also have to rate 30 write-ups during the same time frame. Guest members are not required to submit an idea or pay an annual membership fee. However, as mentioned before, they can only access investment opportunities with a 50-day delay. For most value investing ideas, the delay is not a problem.

# MicroCap Club

MicroCapClub (Microcapclub.com) is an exclusive club for investors interested in small and micro capitalization companies. It was founded by Ian Cassel, a professional micro cap investor. Like other exclusive clubs, members share and discuss various investment ideas with each other. The admission requires an investment idea submission to be approved by the club. This is done to admit only serious and knowledgeable members who can be valuable to the club. There is no requirement as to a number of ideas that have to be submitted but members must be active.

While some members of MicroCapClub may also be members of other exclusive clubs like Value Investors Club or SumZero, they are a different group of investors. They tend to be serious individual investors and professional investors. By professional, I mean ones who make a living by investing their own money, not third-party money managers.

The reason why most mutual fund or hedge fund managers are not interested in micro cap stocks is because they have too much money under management. Micro cap stocks are too small to accommodate their needs. They need big and liquid stocks.

Micro cap stocks are perfect for individual investors with limited funds. They can take advantage of mispriced companies in the micro cap space, which is ignored by the majority of the investment industry. This is exactly what MicroCapClub tries to exploit. The club also offers a public blog open to anyone.

# Seeking Alpha

Seeking Alpha (Seekingalpha.com) is a research platform with insight and analysis provided by investors and industry experts instead of sell-side analysts. The site was founded by David Jackson, a former sell-side analyst with Morgan Stanley, in 2004.

Seeking Alpha has more than 10,000 contributing authors who write about various investment topics including individual stocks. When researching a particular company, I always check to see if someone has written an article or analysis about the company for Seeking Alpha.

Although the site is a research platform, it can also be used to generate investment ideas. You can handpick particular contributors and follow them. Then, every time they submit articles to Seeking Alpha, you will be notified through e-mail. There are all kinds of contributing authors. Some focus on specific sectors while others specialize in particular investment styles like special situations, deep value, or dividend investing.

A lot of the information is accessible free of charge. Recently, the company introduced Seeking Alpha PRO, which is a premium service ($2,400 per year) that allows subscribers early access to the best long and short ideas as well as access to the best research on small and mid caps.

# Form 13F

Institutional managers with $100 million or more in qualifying assets under management must file Form 13F with the SEC. This is a quarterly form that must be filed within 45 days of the end of each quarter. You can gain access to these forms through EDGAR. Also, the website Dataroma.com compiles information from Form 13F filings and lists it in an organized format.

Form 13F reveals what various money managers hold in their portfolios. This is a great way to find investment ideas. Most professional money managers peek at each others' 13F filings. In investing, copying is widespread even though many would not admit to it.

Because there are so many institutions that file Form 13F with the SEC, it is simply not possible and practical to follow all of them. The key is to build a list of money managers that you want to follow. If you want to see mine, visit Classicvalueinvestors.com/resources.

When compiling your own list, you need to keep some things in mind. The disclosure requirements are only for domestic exchanges. Managers are not required to disclose international holdings. This means that if you choose managers who invest internationally, you will not see their full portfolios. Also, short positions are not disclosed. Consequently, it is easier to follow managers that mainly place long bets. Finally, looking at 13F filings from short-term players is useless because by the time the form is filed, they might have already exited the positions. It is best to follow long-term investors who hold investment positions for years, invest in domestic markets, and do not short stocks.

# GuruFocus

Accessing Form 13F filings from money managers is free. The problem is that some investors do not know who to follow and also, they find EDGAR's website clumsy and not very user friendly. GuruFocus (Gurufocus.com) solves this problem for you for $349 per year.

GuruFocus, as the name implies, focuses on gurus or superstar investors such as Bill Ackman, Bruce Berkowitz, Mohnish Pabrai, and Seth Klarman. The site displays the gurus' buys and sells in a readable format. You don't have to compare 13F filings from several quarters to see if a manager added or subtracted from an investment position. The tedious work is done for you.

If you cannot or do not want to pay the subscription fee, you can still benefit from the website. Without the subscription, you can still see gurus' buys and sells, but with a 90-day delay. In other words, the most recent 13F filings are not incorporated into the presentations. However, you can simply take the names of the gurus that interest you and search for their most recent 13F filings in EDGAR.

In addition to publishing gurus' buys and sells, the site also contains many articles discussing publicly traded companies. Like Seeking Alpha, GuruFocus relies on contributing authors for content. This is a great way to generate investment ideas. Often, authors like to write about companies that are their favorite gurus' picks.

# Market Folly

Market Folly (Marketfolly.com) is a website that takes the analysis of 13F filings a little bit further. GuruFocus shows you the names of the companies that gurus are buying or selling but does not provide any explanation behind why they chose to buy or sell. Market Folly publishes *Hedge Fund Wisdom*, a quarterly newsletter ($399.99 per year for four issues) that tracks 25 of the most prominent money managers.

Each newsletter issue is almost 100 pages long. There is a one-page commentary of what changed and why in a particular manager's portfolio. Then, there is an updated list of positions directly from the corresponding 13F filing.

Because these managers hold many individual securities, the discussion about particular companies is limited; otherwise, each issue would contain thousands of pages and would cost thousands of dollars.

With that being said, each issue does contain a detailed analysis on a couple of stocks that the editor found worthy of discussing in depth.

Outside of the *Hedge Fund Wisdom* newsletter, the Market Folly site also contains articles and links to articles that mention investment opportunities to consider.

# Schedules 13D and 13G

Aperson or group that acquires more than five percent of any class of a company's shares must file either Schedule 13D or 13G with the SEC within 10 days of the transaction. The idea behind the filing is to show the public who the large shareholders are.

Schedule 13D is a longer form than 13G. In order to be able to file 13G, the filer has to demonstrate that the investment is only passive. Schedule 13D is used by activist investors who are looking to push for changes.

Schedule 13D requires the filer to disclose the purpose of the transaction. This is the most important piece of information because it shows you whether the shares were purchased for a hostile takeover, proxy battle or some other purpose, such as undervaluation.

SEC's EDGAR allows you to search for filings based on the type of form. Choose SD-13D or SD-13G and you will have plenty of companies to study. If you want to follow smaller money managers, 13D filings and 13G filings might be the only way because if they have less than $100 million under management, they are not required to file Form 13F.

However, if they own more than five percent of any company, they are still required to file either 13D or 13G.

Every month, I check to see if the money managers I follow have filed any 13D filings or 13G filings.

# Shareholder Letters

Money managers communicate with their investors through shareholder or partner letters. Many of them write about individual investment ideas and sometimes include present and past positions. Reading their shareholder letters is a great source for finding your own investments. Remember, they spent resources finding them for their investors and you can simply read about them for free.

You might wonder how you can get access to shareholder letters if you are not a client. Well, in addition to allocating capital, money managers also have to advertise their services, but government regulation puts various restrictions on them. For example, hedge funds cannot advertise freely. They are required to have password-protected websites.

Consequently, by growing a reader base for their letters, they are able to expose themselves to potential clients. They are always looking for new investors. Ask the managers that you follow if you can be added to the distribution list.

Also, there are plenty of money managers that make their letters available on their websites without requiring any registration. They include investors such as Warren Buffett, Martin J. Whitman, and Howard Marks. For a list of letters that I read, visit Classicvalueinvestors.com/resources.

# Insider Buys

**"**Insiders might sell their shares for any number of reasons, but they buy them for only one: they think the price will rise."

—Peter Lynch

All the directors, officers, and owners of more than 10 percent of a company's shares have to file Form 4 to show any buy and sell orders on the open market and the exercising of the company's stock options. The filing has to be submitted within two business days from the end of the day the transaction took place.

Before they file Form 4, they must file Form 3. They only have to file it once. Then, the changes in share ownership are shown on Form 4. Form 5 is an annual statement that they have to file to show their ownership interest.

You can access Form 4 filings by going directly to SEC's EDGAR or by using various websites. There are many websites that are free and do a good job of displaying buy and sell transactions in an easy-to-read format. Insidercow.com is one example.

When analyzing insider buys, pay attention to significant buys in relation to what the insiders already own. Also, it is always better when more than just one insider makes the buys. If it is just one, then it might be because the person just got hired by the company and is required to own some shares.

# Buybacks

When a company buys back its shares the total number of shares are reduced. As a result, the ownership interest of the existing shareholders increases. If an overvalued company were to buy back its stock, it would be a poor use of cash. However, when undervalued companies buy back their stock, the shareholders benefit. Consequently, as a stock researcher, you should pay attention to stock buybacks because they may lead you to companies whose management thinks that their stock is undervalued.

Stock buybacks are announced through press releases. Because there are no forms that have to be filed with the SEC, they are harder to find. You need to either do keyword searches, read press releases, or pay someone to do it for you.

One thing to keep in mind is that just because a company announces a buyback program does not mean that it will be executed. Some companies abandon the program without any announcement and the only way for you to find out whether the buyback took place is to examine the balance sheet and income statement for the number of shares outstanding. This is time consuming.

Fortunately, there is a newsletter that makes your life easier. David Fried is the editor of *The Buyback Letter* (Buybackletter.com), in which he analyzes buybacks and buyback companies in order to offer recommendations about companies that he thinks will increase in price. The cost is $195 per year.

# Twitter

There are thousands of investors sharing investment ideas with each other on Twitter. Many of the money managers that you already follow through shareholder letters, 13F filings, or 13D filings most likely have Twitter accounts. Follow them on Twitter to see what stocks they discuss. Also, while you might not be able to get through to them on the phone, you might be able to ask them questions on Twitter.

Twitter is literally a gold mine for investing ideas. Let's say you follow Ian Cassel, the founder of MicroCapClub. You can visit his profile and look through the people that he follows. Then, you can follow them also because most of them are investors interested in micro cap investing and they talk about it on a daily basis.

If you are interested in finding investment opportunities in distressed debt or deep value investing, go to Twitter and search for these topics. Look at the profiles of people that show up in the results to figure out whether they are talking about topics that will help you find potential investment opportunities. You will be amazed at the types of contacts you can make this way.

Twitter is also great when you are conducting due diligence on a particular company. You can find competitors, suppliers, and other investors that can help you in studying the company. You can also find out what customers are saying.

# StockTwits

StockTwits (Stocktwits.com) is a fantastic social media platform that allows investors to share investment ideas with each other. The site was co-founded by Howard Lindzon and Soren Macbeth in 2008.

Lindzon thought that Twitter could be fantastic for stocks so they created StockTwits using the same technology that runs Twitter. Users can share comments about particular companies by placing $ in front of the ticker symbol, like $AAPL. Then, the tweets are categorized according to the ticker symbols.

You can use StockTwits to find investment ideas and conduct due diligence on your stocks. To find investment ideas, you need to build a network of investors to follow. This is as easy as using regular Twitter. Once you specify what type of investor you are (value investor, trader, etc.), then StockTwits recommends various users for you to follow.

When conducting due diligence, you can search StockTwits by using ticker symbols or companies' names.

# Facebook

J ust like Twitter, Facebook can be a place to generate investment ideas. Nearly everyone has a Facebook account so there are plenty of investors talking about stocks. You can find discussions on individual companies within people's posts, groups, or pages.

There are Facebook groups dedicated to all kinds of specialized topics within the field of investing. Find them, join them, and benefit from them. If you can't find what you are looking for, start your own group and recruit members to it.

I see a lot of people setting up Facebook pages instead of websites or in addition to websites. They are easy to set up and you can quickly invite friends. With websites, you have to figure out how to build them, buy a domain, get hosting, and wait forever to generate traffic. With Facebook pages, life is a lot easier. You can set it up in minutes without any coding skills.

Many investment bloggers also set up Facebook pages to supplement their websites and grow their audiences.

# Magic Formula Investing

Magic Formula Investing (Magicformulainvesting.com) is a quantitative stock screen based on Joel Greenblatt's book, *The Little Book that Beats the Market.* Greenblatt is also the co-founder of Value Investors Club, which was discussed at the beginning of this book, and he is a part owner of Magicformulainvesting.com.

The Magic Formula Investing screen is based on the idea that cheap stocks of good quality companies tend to beat the market. The screen uses the S&P Compustat database to screen US-listed stocks to find ones with low price-to-earnings ratios (cheap stocks) and high returns on capital (good quality companies). Financial and utility stocks are not included because of their unique financial reporting requirements.

When using the screen, you can search by company size and focus on small or large cap stocks. Also, you can choose how many companies you want the screen to display for every search.

Once you have a list of companies, you can study them one by one to figure out which ones meet your investment criteria. One strategy is to simply buy the stocks from the search without studying individual companies, but I like to know what I am buying rather than simply relying on a computer to do the thinking for me.

# MagicDiligence

MagicDiligence (Magicdiligence.com) and Magic Formula Investing go hand in hand. Magic Formula Investing is simply a screen that generates a list of stocks for you without any analysis. MagicDiligence is a completely separate website that provides analysis on stocks generated by the Magic Formula Investing screen.

It is important to point out that Joel Greenblatt has no connection to MagicDiligence. An investor named Steve Alexander founded MagicDiligence after reading *The Little Book that Beats the Market*. He was impressed with the book and the Magic Formula Investing screen but realized that some of the stocks generated by the screen have problems such as high debt, fad products, accounting issues, and so forth.

He thought that the screen was a great starting point for further stock research but wanted to throw out the problem companies and focus only on the good ones. Consequently, he started MagicDiligence for this purpose.

The membership to MagicDiligence costs $12 per month which is relatively cheaper than other services. It is worth the money for investors who use the Magic Formula Investing screen.

# Google and Yahoo Groups

**B**oth Google and Yahoo allow people to start discussion groups. There are thousands of groups on all types of topics including investing. Although the popularity of some Google and Yahoo groups has declined with the invention of Facebook and other social media sites, many are still going strong.

Two Yahoo groups worth checking out are Magic Formula Investing and Chucks_Angels. Magic Formula Investing is a group that discusses stocks from the Magic Formula Investing screen that was discussed in a previous section. Chucks_Angels is a group is for fans of Berkshire Hathaway, Warren Buffett, and Charlie Munger. Members discuss investment opportunities in the US and internationally.

One Google group dedicated to value investing is Deep Value. It was started by John Chew as a supplement to his educational website, Csinvesting.org.

Many of the groups are kept private meaning that you have to be approved to see the content. The reason for this is to prevent spam. The public groups are mostly useless because they contain mostly advertisements and links to pornography. So, don't get discouraged when you cannot see the content of private groups. Join first. They are free. Then, if you don't like it, you can cancel your membership.

# Meetup

With the invention of social media along with other changes in our society, many people have become increasingly isolated. Even though we may have lots of friends on Facebook, we may not have as much personal contact as we would like. Meetup.com is a place where people go to use the Internet to connect and meet in person.

The site was co-founded by Scott Heiferman and four others after the 9/11 terrorist attack. In the wake of the crisis, Heiferman began talking with a lot of his neighbors and strangers on the street. He realized that people needed a way to find and form local communities where they can talk and interact with real people in person.

Today, Meetup is an online platform for organizing local get-togethers. You can go there to find all kinds of groups from parenting to surfing. By joining and attending investing groups, you will be exposed to many investment ideas.

Obviously, when it comes to investing groups, bigger cities like New York or Chicago have more to offer, and therefore, will have more Meetup groups than smaller cities.

If you cannot find a group in your city, consider starting one. It is easy. It costs $10 per month to organize a group. You can charge members a small fee each meeting to cover the cost. You can meet at your house, office, church, or any other place that can accommodate groups of people.

# Message Boards

Message boards are places on the Internet where investors of particular stocks engage in discussions. For example, Apple and Microsoft have their own separate boards. While many people think of message boards as research tools, they are also places to find investment ideas.

When I research a particular company, I always visit several message boards to see what other investors have to say about the subject company. Then, when I find a poster that continues to write knowledgeable and insightful comments, I usually click on his profile to see what other companies he comments on. This way, I get to learn about other investment opportunities.

Sometimes, I contact that person. After the initial contact, I try to get the person on the phone to learn more information about the company and any other companies that he likes.

The three message boards that you should use are Yahoo Message Board, Investors Hub, and Stockhouse. Yahoo Message boards are great for US-listed stocks while

Stockhouse is the number one place for Canadian companies trading on the TSX and TSX Venture Exchange. Stockhouse also allows investors to comment on US stocks, but most US investors use other message boards.

# Forums

Investing forums are places that give investors a chance to have active conversations about specialized topics within investing. There are many investing forums but unfortunately many of them are useless and dominated by spammers, stock promoters, clueless investors, and fraudulent individuals. However, there are several forums that do have valuable discussions about investing opportunities. They include:

- **American Association of Individual Investors**
    - Aaii.com/boards

- **Corner of Berkshire and Fairfax**
    - Cornerofberkshireandfairfax.ca/forum

- **GuruFocus**
    - Gurufocus.com/forum

- **Old School Value Forum**
    - Oldschoolvalue.com/forum

- **Reddit Security Analysis**
  - Reddit.com/r/securityanalysis

- **Warren Buffett Forum**
  - Warrenbuffettforum.com

- **Silicon Investor**
  - Siliconinvestor.com

- **Microcap Kitchen Canadian Stocks**
  - Part of the Silicon Investor Forum site; found most easily by searching on Google

# Shopping Malls

The majority of people on Wall Street find investment ideas by reading reports written by sell-side analysts. They would never bother kicking tires themselves because their ties and suits would get dirty.

Peter Lynch, who ran Fidelity Magellan fund from 1977 to 1990, generated an incredible investment record during that time period. He used to get his investment ideas by visiting shopping malls. It makes sense because this is where people spend their money and our economy is mostly consumer driven.

You can do the same thing. Go to the mall and watch what bags people are carrying to find out what stores they are shopping at. Visit individual stores. Take note of the types of products they are selling. Notice if there are any new products being carried. Talk to the salespeople about the types of products people are buying and the types of products that are going to be sold in the future.

Barely anyone is doing this type of research. You will have an advantage. You might discover great stock picks well before anyone on Wall Street notices them.

# Spouse and Kids

Grown men have the attitude that picking investments is complicated and should be left for adults
and professionals. While that might be partially
true when it comes to performing due diligence and analysis,
talking with your spouse and kids might be a great source of
investment ideas.

Peter Lynch found many of his ideas by talking with his
family. He learned about Apple because one of his kids had
an Apple product. Teenagers know what is popular. They
are aware of various brands. They knew about iPods well
before Wall Street caught on to it.

I remember watching Mad Money with Jim Cramer years
ago. He had learned from his kids how great iPods were.
Originally, he thought that once someone had one, there
would be no reason to buy another one. He was wrong. His
kids taught him that an iPod was an accessory and people
would buy more than one because they wanted different
colors.

So, don't ignore your spouse or kids when it comes to investing. Talk to them. Learn from them. Let them help you find investment opportunities to research further.

# LikeFolio

Peter Lynch was famous for "invest in what you know" types of companies by observing the types of brands that people liked and talked about. This is why he found some of his best investment ideas by talking to his family and walking the mall.

LikeFolio (Likefolio.com) is a website that tries to reproduce the same investing style by using social media. By connecting your Twitter or Facebook account to the site, LikeFolio combs through your network of friends and contacts to look for mentions and likes of brands and products. Then, it links them to publicly traded companies associated with these brands and products.

The idea behind this is to help you discover investment opportunities early by showing you customers' enthusiasm before it turns into revenues and profits on Wall Street.

# Consumer Reports

Consumers are constantly being bombarded with marketing and advertising messages about how great particular products are. Consumer Reports (Consumerreports.org) is a non-profit organization that publishes reviews and comparisons of consumer products and services in order to help consumers make better choices. In addition to online services and mobile apps, a monthly newsletter, magazines, and books and guides are also available in print.

The organization follows an ad-free subscription-based model in order to maintain its impartiality. It also pays for the products that it tests and reviews instead of accepting free product samples. Because the organization has been around since 1936, it has a great reputation. It has more than 7 million subscribers.

Whatever it says about the products and services, their opinions can directly affect consumers' buying habits and therefore, the success of the companies that supply the products. Reading their reviews and reports can be another way to generate more investment ideas.

# Industry Conventions

Practically all industries from mining to electronics have industry conventions where companies introduce new products, source suppliers, network, and spy on competitors. Attending specific conferences can be a great way to find investment ideas especially because few investors do it. Again, they would rather get hot tips from their brokers than attend industry conferences.

The best approach to take is to study the industry before you attend so that you are not overwhelmed by so much new information. While attending a convention, watch the crowd. Which booths have the most people and why? Is it because a new product was introduced or did the company hire a performer to entertain the crowd?

Talk to people to learn about new products, new companies, or problems that face the industry. Find out which companies are shaping the future. Talk to individual companies at their booths. Let them tell you how their products solve customers' needs. Maybe there will be some customers at the convention who can provide some insight about the company's performance.

By attending industry conventions, you can gain a wealth of information long before the investment community learns about it.

# Industry Publications and Websites

Nearly every industry is served by trade publications and industry-specific websites that profile companies, cover news of current developments, and provide highly specialized information. They write about products, regulation, and various industry issues. They interview CEOs and chief product developers. They know who the movers and shakers are.

Read their work. Reach out to them. Ask them questions. Find out where the industry is going, what kind of problems it is facing, and who will provide the solutions. Learn about the kinds of products that are being developed to solve particular problems. Find out how big the market is for particular products.

If you do this kind of work, then you might find a company with low or nonexistent revenues but a bright future. While everyone else will see the company as a loser based on the weak financials, you will appreciate the forthcoming impact of the company's new product on its industry.

# CEOs

When researching companies, especially small ones, you should always try to talk to the company's management which includes the CEO. Obviously, with the large companies, it is almost never possible to talk to the CEO but with smaller companies, I almost always get to talk to them.

This is helpful because they can explain to you how their business works in a way that is easier to understand than reading an annual report. Also, while you have the CEO on the phone, you should ask about whether he or she knows of other investment opportunities. Ask about his favorite suppliers or clients that are doing well.

There were several times when I found investment opportunities like this. For example, one time a company whose stock I owned purchased an asset from another company. I called the CEO and asked about the transaction and what he thought about the company that sold them the asset. He spoke highly of their management and the assets that they kept. So, I researched that company and ended up buying the stock because the valuation was a no-brainer.

CEOs know a lot about what is going on in their industry. Of course, sometimes they might not give you useful information, but when they do mention a particular investment opportunity, it is worth researching it further.

# Investor Presentations

U nderstanding any company's business takes time. Usually, when you read the company's description, you do not learn much. Most of the time, you have to read the annual report and browse through the company's website to start understanding the business.

Companies often publish investor presentations on their websites as part of the investor relations section. This is where they try to describe their business to you and explain why you should invest in it. Sometimes, they include a peer-to-peer comparison showing how the company's valuation stacks up against its competitors.

By looking at investor presentations, you might learn about other companies that are as cheap or cheaper than your subject company. This practice of peer-to-peer comparisons is common among gold mining companies.

With that being said, other industries use it, too, but it is at the discretion of the management. I was recently researching a hotel REIT and discovered several other cheaply priced REITS listed in a company-to-company comparison that was part of the investor presentation.

# Company Tours

One of the ways publicly traded companies expose themselves to the investment community is by hosting company tours. They invite investors, newsletter writers, and analysts to show them the operations.

If you have a chance to attend some of these tours, you should definitely take advantage of it. Not only do you get to learn about the specific company, but you will also learn about its competitors. In addition, you will meet other investors who have similar taste in investments.

After the official tour, the companies feed investors to make sure they do not leave with empty stomachs. This is when you can learn a lot. The most common question investors ask each other is "What else do you like?" The last time I went on a tour, I left with four investment ideas. People who invest for a living enjoy telling you about the stocks that they own.

# Non-Deal Road Shows

The majority of public companies have investor relations departments. However, the smaller ones tend to outsource a lot of those responsibilities to third-party investor relations firms. To serve their clients better, these firms sometimes organize non-deal road shows where they travel with the companies' management to large cities to introduce them to investors, analysts, and newsletter writers. The term "non-deal" refers to the idea that nothing is being offered for sale. Instead, the purpose is simply to meet and share information.

Let the companies you follow know that you are interested in meeting their management whenever they visit your city or a city near you. Contact investor relations firms and have them add you to their investor databases. They are always looking for investors to introduce to the management teams that they represent.

For example, Torrey Hills Capital is an investor relations firm from California representing small firms that trade on the NYSE, AMEX, and over the counter in the US, and on the TSX, TSX-V, and CNQ in Canada. They frequently bring their clients to Chicago for non-deal road shows and they always let me know about the dates and types of companies they are bringing.

# Investor Relations Firms

Thousands of companies use investor relations firms to expose themselves to the investment community. Tracking and establishing relationships with various investor relations firms can expose you to profitable investment ideas. Of the companies they represent, they know which are good buys and which are not.

With that being said, when listening to investor relations firms, you have to be careful. You always have to do your due diligence. These firms are nothing but stock promoters. While there are many reputable firms that truly want to help their clients gain exposure, there are also bad apples who try to push stock prices high in order to dump their shares.

I have a few investor relations firms that I follow. I learned about them while studying various companies. For example, while I was conducting due diligence on InfuSystem Holdings, I learned about Lytham Partners, which represented the company. They were professional and knowledgeable when answering my questions. Since that day, I have followed them and continue to pay attention to the companies they serve.

Another example is Torrey Hills Capital which is an investor relations firm out of California. They invited me to attend a tour of three mines belonging to Scorpio Gold Corporation in Nevada. On the tour, I had a chance to become acquainted with one of the firm's employees and we chatted about various companies the firm represents. Now, I always look through the list of companies that they represent. Do I like all of them? Of course not. I let them expose me to possibilities and I do my own work to decide which ones are worthy of my investment.

Other firms that I follow include Acorn Management Partners; EVC Group; Hayden Investor Relations; Porter, LeVay and Rose; and Cameron Associates. All of them specialize in representing small cap companies.

# Independent Research Firms

Traditionally, equity research was provided by Wall Street's investment banks. This is called sell-side research because it is produced by the firms that are hired to sell securities to the investment community. The cost of that research was covered by high commission costs.

With the advent of electronic trading and discount brokers, everything changed. Wall Street firms lost their monopoly on equity research. Many independent research firms were born.

There are thousands of independent research firms and they are all different. Some specialize in particular sectors such as pharmaceutical, technology, or defense. Others focus on particular investment styles.

While they all differ, one thing is the same—they rely on subscription-based models. This is understandable because they do not get to charge commission like Wall Street firms so they have to make money in other ways.

Some of the most popular independent research firms include Morningstar, Argus Research, Edison Investment Research, Schaeffer's Investment Research, Russell Investments, and Zacks Investment Research.

# Blogs

While you have to pay money for independent research, you can read investment blogs for free. Some people are passionate about investing and they start blogs to share their thoughts and investment ideas with like-minded individuals.

Some of the blogs that I follow are:

- Alex Bossert's Thoughts on Value Investing
- BeyondProxy
- Bronte Capital
- Old School Value
- OTC Adventures

For the rest of my list, visit:

Classicvalueinvestors.com/resources

The reason why I do not want to paste my entire list here is because by the time you read this book, half of the blogs might be gone. The turnover is high because maintaining a blog takes time and there is no compensation unless you are using it to promote yourself. Consequently, bloggers get tired, run out of material to write about, get jobs, or simply move on with their lives.

Despite that, you should build a list of blogs that you follow and update it every six months.

# Start Your Own Blog

So far, everything has been about where to go to find investment ideas. Why not let them come to you? When you start an investment blog, you can attract other investors who will bring you ideas. After I started my Classic Value Investors blog, I expanded my network tremendously. I have thousands of investors in my Constant Contact list. Every week, someone writes to me about an investment idea.

With your own investment blog, you can write about companies, interview CEOs, review books, and record videos. If you create good content, people will find you and discuss investment ideas with you. Also, you can include a forum where people discuss investment ideas with each other.

There are many benefits of having your own blog. How do you think I get invited to company tours and road shows? Having a website opens up new opportunities for you. When you call the companies for information, they take you a little bit more seriously when you have a public platform. They return your calls.

With that being said, if you decide to start a blog, do it the right way. Get your own domain, buy an attractive template, and use WordPress as your platform. It does not take that much to make your website look inviting. Unfortunately, so many bloggers have terrible-looking websites that are difficult to navigate.

# The Manual of Ideas

The *Manual of Ideas* (Manualofideas.com) is a monthly publication that includes information on various value investing investment ideas. The site was founded by John Mihaljevic who is also the author of *The Manual of Ideas: The Proven Framework for Finding the Best Value Investments.*

In addition to this site, Mihaljevic also started a portfolio of other websites which provide great resources for value investors. The portfolio of websites includes:

- BeyondProxy
- The Moat Report: Asia
- ValueConferences
- GreatInvestors.TV
- Undiscovered.PM

Mihaljevic also created the Value Investing Podcast which will be discussed in the next section.

# Podcasts

While there are many investment blogs that discuss individual investment ideas, there are not that many podcasts that do so. Most podcasts on investing provide only general information. However, sometimes they will include interviews with successful investors, which gives you an opportunity to build a database of investors to follow.

The investing podcasts that I recommend are:

- **Value Investing Podcast**
  - Valuepodcast.com

- **The Investors Podcast**
  - Theinvestorspodcast.com

- **The Value Guys**
  - Thevalueguys.com

The Value Investing Podcast is hosted by John Mihaljevic who is a managing editor of *The Manual of Ideas* newsletter. In the podcast, he interviews successful investors.

The Investors Podcast is about studying and analyzing billionaires and is hosted by Preston Pysh and Stig Brodersen. Pysh wrote *Warren Buffett's Three Favorite Books*, and he and Broderson co-authored three other books on investing.

The Value Guys podcast is hosted by two 30-year veteran Wall Street analysts who have electronically altered their voices so as not to be discovered by their employers who would never allow them to talk freely about particular stocks.

# YouTube

I bet you never thought that you could use YouTube to find investment ideas. Think about it from the point of view of a content creator. Let's say I want to conduct a Skype interview with the CEO of a particular company. After I record it, I face a dilemma. How do I place it on my website? I could upload it to my server, which takes up lots of space, I could buy another hosting plan, or I could upload it to YouTube for free.

There are plenty of users who upload content about investment ideas to YouTube. You just have to build your own list of YouTube channels to follow. They include individual investors, investor relations firms, conference providers, and hedge funds.

For example, Tal Davidson, a value investor, did a 30-minute detailed analysis of why he thought Rosetta Stone was undervalued. GuruFocus, which I already described, has a YouTube channel showing you how to use the site to find investment ideas.

YouTube channels worth considering are Edison Investment Research, The Manual of Ideas, Zacks Investment

News, Stock News Now, and Investing News Network. For a full list, visit Classicvalueinvestors.com/resources.

# Scribd

S cribd (Scribd.com) is probably the most unutilized source for finding investment ideas, but it is absolutely fantastic. After hearing about his father's frustration with how long it took to publish his medical research, John R. "Trip" Adler III was inspired to co-found Scribd with his friend Jared Friedman. The site was launched in March 2007.

Scribd is a publishing platform where users can upload all kinds of documents. By documents I mean presentations, letters, e-books, white papers, and newsletters. Mostly they are in PDF format, but they can also be in Word, PowerPoint and Excel. I have used Scribd several times to upload PDF documents that I wanted to embed on my blog.

Remember how I told you that reading shareholder letters is a great way to generate investment opportunities but you have to request to be on the list? Well, you can search for those letters on Scribd. Search for the manager's or hedge fund's name. It is likely that someone has uploaded the letter to Scribd. Remember, many managers do not mind because they want to be exposed.

What about finding issues of your favorite newsletter? Again, someone may have uploaded slightly outdated issues that still contain actionable investment ideas.

# SlideShare

SlideShare (Slideshare.net) is similar to Scribd but for presentations. The site was started in October 2006 by Rashmi Sinha, Jon Boutelle, and Amit Ranjan, and was acquired by LinkedIn in May 2012. Because SlideShare is a slide-hosting service, you can think of it as the YouTube for slideshows.

The site is used by all types of people from the investment industry such as public companies, investor relations firms, activists, money managers, and individual investors. Public companies can use it to upload investor presentations. Investor relations firms can use it to expose their client companies. Activists can use it to make the case for being aggressive toward a particular company. Finally, money managers and individual investors can use it to share investment ideas.

Like Scribd, you must find people that you want to follow. If you like micro cap investing, you should follow Ian Cassel from MicroCapClub. If you prefer mainstream investing, then you should consider The Motley Fool. Build your own network on SlideShare to find actionable investment ideas.

# Newsletters

nvestment newsletters can definitely save you some time when it comes to investment research, assuming, of course, you subscribe to ones that fit your investment strategy.

Four newsletters that are useful:

## Graham and Doddsville

- www8.gsb.columbia.edu/valueinvesting/resources/newsletters
- Grahamanddoddsville.net

This newsletter is written by students of Columbia Business School and it is free.

## Value Investor Insight

- Valueinvestorinsight.com

*Value Investor Insight* includes interviews with money managers, their investment philosophies, and stocks that they like. The cost is $349 per year.

## Deep Value Letter

- Deepvalue.com

Deep Value Letter focuses on deep value investment opportunities. It costs $195 per year.

## Value Investor Confidential

- Valueinvestorconfidential.com

This newsletter includes interviews with money managers along with investment ideas. The cost is $499 per year.

# Value Investing Congress

Value Investing Congress has been referred to as the "Super Bowl of Value Investing." It was founded in 2004 by Whitney Tilson and John Schwartz to bring together the community of serious value investors. It is a two-day event that takes place in Las Vegas during the first half of the year and New York during the second part of the year.

The congress features approximately two dozen speakers who are some of the best value investors in the world such as Bill Ackman, David Einhorn, and Joel Greenblatt. They engage the audience in lengthy presentations on value investing strategies and actionable investment ideas. The event also provides plenty of opportunities to network with other value investors.

The cost to attend Value Investing Congress is several thousand dollars. Those who cannot attend the event can purchase some of the content in various formats through "Value Access" on the Value Investing Congress website at a fraction of the cost.

# Annual Meetings

Most of the publicly traded companies host annual meetings so that shareholders can have a chance to talk with the management. By attending such events, you can meet and network with other investors who are invested alongside you in particular companies. If they own XYZ company with you, then you might learn about another investment opportunity from them.

If you own technology companies, attend the meetings to meet other technology investors. If you want to meet other value investors, go to annual meetings that they attend. The following four annual meetings are very popular among value investors:

**Berkshire Hathaway Annual Meeting**

Thousands of investors attend it each year to hear Warren Buffett and Charlie Munger speak.

**Fairfax Financial Annual Meeting**

Investors attend Fairfax Financial's annual meeting to listen to Prem Watsa.

## Daily Journal Corporation Annual Meeting

Charlie Munger is the chairman of the board of Daily Journal Corporation and his followers try not to miss the annual meeting.

## Sears Holdings Annual Meeting

Eddie Lampert, a well known value investor, is running Sears with the intention of successfully turning it around.

# Investment Conferences

B ecause of the large size of the investment industry, there are a lot of investment conferences designed to meet the appetite for investment information and actionable investment ideas. The following are some of the best investment conferences attended by serious investors:

- **The Sohn Conference**
  - Sohnconference.org
- **Boston Investment Conference**
  - Bostoninvestmentconference.com
- **Grant's Conference**
  - Grantspub.com/conferences
- **Santangel's Investor Forum**
  - Santangelsreview.com/forum
- **UVa Investing Conference**
  - Darden.virginia.edu/uvic
- **Great Investors' Best Ideas Investment Symposium**
  - Gibidallas.com
- **Harbor Investment Conference**
  - Theharbor.org/hic

# Virtual Conferences

Physical investment conferences are great but you have to attend them in person, which can be difficult if you have other responsibilities like a day job that is not investing. Also, it costs money to pay for the ticket, hotel, and transportation. Virtual conferences try to deliver the same experience but over the Internet.

ValueConferences (Valueconferences.com) is a series of online investment conferences for value investors. It was founded by the same individuals that founded *The Manual of Ideas*. The series of events includes:

- Wide-Moat Investing Summit
- Asian Investing Summit
- Best Ideas
- European Investing Summit

To deliver the virtual conferences, the organizers assembled a team of global investors who provide insight and investment ideas to the participants.

Other virtual conferences that are organized by different people include Virtualinvestorconferences.com and Retailinvestorconferences.com.

# Investment Clubs

There are investment clubs all over the country where small groups of individuals meet on a regular basis to share investment knowledge and ideas with each other. Some clubs pool their money together while others meet only for informational purposes.

The National Association of Investors Corporation, which is also known as BetterInvesting (Betterinvesting.org), is a non-profit organization headquartered in Michigan. It was founded in 1951. In addition to providing investment education resources, the organization helps investors form investment clubs and provides access to existing clubs.

The membership reached 400,000 members in 1998 (near the peak of the dot-com bubble) and fell to 39,000 in 2012. With the number of resources available online, it is facing lots of competition so the membership is not easy to grow.

If you live in a city that has a good investment club, you should consider checking it out. Otherwise, you may want to start one yourself.

# Books

Warren Buffett always said that in order to be a good investor, you have to read a lot. Although books may not be the first place you think of when you are looking for ways to generate investment ideas, they can be a great source. It really depends on the particular book.

For example, when I wrote my first book, *Why Are We So Clueless about the Stock Market?*, I included four case studies which were actionable investment ideas. They were Burlington Northern Santa Fe, Thor Industries, Wells Fargo, and Moody's Investors Service. Over the years, all of them performed well. Burlington Northern Santa Fe was bought by Berkshire Hathaway at a profit. Thor Industries and Wells Fargo doubled. Moody's Investors Service tripled. Years ago, I read a book, *The Forever Portfolio* by James Altucher and it included a list of fantastic companies that I made money on.

Obviously, the problem with finding investment ideas in books is that they may become outdated. While this is true, you can still learn a lot from them. I wrote about Moody's and Wells Fargo in my book and I originally learned about them from other books. Then, when the financial crisis hit, I already knew which companies to pursue.

If you are looking for a book that provides you with investment ideas every year, take a look at *The 100 Best Stocks to Buy in 20XX* year series by Peter Sander and Scott Bobo. As the name states, the series features 100 companies each year and the authors take current economic events into account when compiling their stock picks.

# Competitors

When studying companies, you should take the time to talk to their competitors especially when you are dealing with small cap companies. The companies disclose their competitors in the 10-K filings for the public to see.

Call the competitors and ask them how various companies in the industry compare to each other. Find out which ones are hated (usually the strong ones) and which ones are ignored. Ask them if they had a choice to purchase one other than themselves, which one it would be.

Their answers will give you an idea whether you are researching the right company or whether you should look at one of its competitors instead.

Competitors know a lot of information about each other. If you gain their trust, they will tell you things that you would have a hard time finding out on your own.

# Suppliers

You can obtain similar information from the company's suppliers. While the competitors are easy to locate, finding suppliers is bit trickier. You have to be creative. You can ask the company for a list of suppliers or figure out what the company needs and look for companies that supply it.

When you contact the suppliers, ask them about the industry that they serve. Find out the dominant players. Which companies are growing the most? Which ones have the best products? Are there any companies that are developing something new that will change the industry?

Like competitors, suppliers know information about their clients that no one else does. They know if someone is honest, pays their bills on time, or operates a legitimate business. Their insights can point you to the right investment opportunities.

# Hated Industries

All industries go through cycles of popularity. At any given time, there will be some industries that the majority of investors love and some that they hate. When an industry is hot, it is unlikely that investors will be willing to give you a good deal on stocks within that industry. However, when an industry is out of favor, it becomes fertile ground for bargain hunters.

Pay attention to which industries are unpopular. If you read the newspapers and Yahoo Finance, and watch CNBC, you will quickly learn what everybody hates. For example, as of the date of this book, the financial media has no hope for the gold mining industry. I have never seen an industry that has been hated more than the gold mining industry. It is amazing.

Also, the price of oil has collapsed over the last year or so. The stocks of companies in the oil and gas industry have been decimated, creating a lot of hate for these stocks and for the entire industry. By studying individual industries when they are unpopular, you can find fantastic companies with great businesses and clean balance sheets.

# Hated Countries

The same "hate" philosophy can be applied to countries. When there is hate, there is opportunity. Turn on the TV or open up a newspaper and you will find numerous stories of how particular countries are out of favor.

For example, Greece is hated because they borrowed more money than they can repay. Russia's global reputation has deteriorated due to Vladimir Putin's aggressive posturing. Consequently, investors do not want to touch stocks in these countries with a 10-foot pole.

Their hate and fear is your opportunity. With that being said, I am not saying that you should go out and buy all the stocks in these countries. Be selective. Buy good businesses with great products, wide margins, and protective moats. You can take the time to study and analyze them because everybody else is avoiding them.

# Hated Exchanges

S ince we are on the topic of hate, why not look at hated exchanges? Stock exchanges are also businesses. They try to attract public companies to float their shares on their platforms. To be competitive, they might cater to specific industries or market capitalizations.

For example, the AIM (Alternative Investment Market) exchange in London caters to small capitalization companies. Canada's TSX Venture Exchange caters to mining and oil and gas companies.

As I already mentioned in the previous section, the mining and oil and gas industries are extremely hated because the prices of the products that they are selling declined. Because the TSX Venture Exchange caters to those companies, the entire exchange is hated. It is down more than 80 percent over the last three years.

This is an incredible opportunity. You can find great companies with great assets that are selling for pennies on the dollar. Also, just because the TSX Venture Exchange caters to specific industries does not mean that no other companies are listed there. Approximately a quarter of the companies listed on the TSX Venture Exchange are regular companies. Some of them have great businesses but they are selling cheaply because the entire exchange is hated.

# 52-Week Low Lists

Value investors love looking at 52-week low lists to find bargains because stocks whose prices have reached a 52-week low usually have exhausted shareholders so much that many of them choose to sell without any consideration for the underlying value.

Consequently, you should study the companies on that list one by one in order to see if there are any cheaply priced stocks. Because generating 52-week low lists is purely quantitative, a lot of websites provide them at no charge.

Here are some examples:

- Gurufocus.com/52weeklow.php
- Nasdaq.com/aspx/52-week-high-low.aspx
- Msn.com/en-us/money/stockscreener/52weeklows
- Morningstar.com/highlow/gethighlow.aspx

# 52-Week High Lists

Many value investors know that the place to find good deals is the 52-week low list. However, almost none of them acknowledge that they can also find deals on 52-week high lists. How can that be?

Companies that find themselves on the 52-week low list get sold off by investors because they disappoint them. Even after they stop disappointing them, their stock prices might stay low in a particular range for a long time until something changes.

A company might turn itself around by developing a new product, cutting its cost structure, or replacing a lost customer. As a result, the stock price will recover slightly making it to the 52-week high list for the first time. If you ignore the 52-week high list, you will miss capturing the gains that will follow when others realize what is going on and join the party.

This is exactly how my friend found Silicom Ltd. (SILC). He found it on a 52-week high list at $10 per share after the stock had already doubled. Because the company kept performing well, the stock price kept going up and he benefited tremendously. It went as high as $70 per share. All the other value investors missed it because they ignored the 52-week high lists.

# Screeners

A s you know, there are thousands of publicly traded companies and each one has their own unique story. In a perfect world, you would know them all and this would allow you to pick the best investment opportunities. However, we do not have the resources to be able to study and analyze every single publicly traded company. Therefore, we need shortcuts to point us in the right direction. Screeners are one of these shortcuts.

Screeners can be quantitative or qualitative, but quantitative screens, where a computer searches through thousands of companies to generate a list based on various quantitative variables such as market capitalizations, P/E ratios, or growth rates, are by far the most predominant. Magic Formula Investing is an example of this type of screen. The following is a list of popular screeners.

- **Finviz Screener**
  - Finviz.com/screener.ashx?

- **Google Screener**
  - ○ Google.com/finance/stockscreener

- **Yahoo Screener**
  - ○ Screener.finance.yahoo.com/stocks.html

# Pre-Defined Screens

When using quantitative screens, you need to know what you are looking for. In other words, you have to set the parameters. Some investors want to look at screens that already have popular parameters entered so that they can focus on just studying the companies rather than trying to figure out what to search for. The following is a list of pre-defined screens.

- **Old School Value**
  - o   Oldschoolvalue.com/stock-screener.php

- **CNBC Screens**
  - o   Cnbc.com/stock-screener/

- **The Graham Investor Screens**
  - o   Grahaminvestor.com/screens

- **Stingy Investor Screens**
  - o   Ndir.com/SI/strategy.shtml

# Form 12b-25 – NT 10-Q/K

Publicly traded companies are required to file all sorts of documents with the Securities and Exchange Commission. This includes the filing of Forms 10-Q and 10-K, which represent quarterly and annual reports, respectively.

When companies cannot file them on time, they must file Form 12b-25 with the SEC, which notifies the commission that the filing will be late. Because the filing of this form is a red flag indicating that something might be seriously wrong with the company, it can result in heavy selling of the stock.

When the selling is overdone causing the stock price to decline too much in relation to the underlying value, it can present a buying opportunity. Carefully studying companies that have filed late can be worthwhile.

Although companies are required to file Form 12b-25, you cannot search SEC's EDGAR by that name. Instead, you need to search for the following forms:

"NT 10-K" or "NT 10-Q"

On EDGAR, Form 12b-25 is designated as either NT 10-K or NT 10-Q.

# Form 10-12B — Spinoffs

M any companies have various businesses under their ownership. The management would like the market to assign full value to all of the businesses, but this is not always the case. Consequently, to create shareholder value, the management might decide to spin a business off from its parent company.

Usually, new shares of the newly independent company are created and distributed to the shareholders of the parent company in the form of stock dividends. It is not uncommon for these shareholders to not want the shares. For example, the spinoff company might be too small for them to own it. As a result, the stock price of the spinoff company might be under pressure in the short term until all the unwanted shares are liquidated. These unusually high levels of selling unrelated to the performance of the underlying business create conditions conducive to finding great investment opportunities.

You can find spinoff opportunities by searching EDGAR for filings of the Form 10-12B. This form, called the Initial General Form for Registration of Securities, is required to be filed with the SEC when a public company issues new shares through a spinoff transaction.

Also, you can find a list of spinoffs at Stockspinoffs.com.

# Form S-1 – IPOs

F orm S-1 is required to be filed with the SEC by companies that are going public. You can search for filings of these forms on SEC's EDGAR.

It is hard to find undervalued IPOs because companies are usually taken public when the business fundamentals look great. Also, during the IPO process, the investment bankers heavily promote the stock. Hence, IPOs are referred to as "It's Probably Overpriced." Because of this fact, I usually never invest in IPOs.

However, I like to create a list of IPOs to watch for future disappointments. When IPOs are overhyped, the companies will eventually under deliver on the unreasonably high expectations and the stock price will get hammered. This is when you come in to estimate the value and future prospects in relation to the stock price.

Another strategy is to wait for the lock-up period to expire. When companies go public, the underwriters and insiders enter into an agreement where the insiders are not allowed to sell their shares for a specific period of time—a lock-up period.

When that period is over and the insiders are still not selling the stock, then this might be telling you something— they believe that the stock price is going to increase because of the company's bright future. Hence, studying and analyzing companies whose lock-up period has expired and whose insiders are not selling might be a good use of your time.

# Form DEFC 14A

Publicly traded companies are owned by shareholders who sometimes are not satisfied with the performance of the managers who are operating their companies. Consequently, they might force a change through a proxy fight.

The change may include replacing the management, a spinoff, or returning cash to shareholders. Such shareholders (usually activist investors) may try to solicit votes from other shareholders in order to accumulate enough power to force their agendas. In order to solicit proxy votes, they file Form DEFC 14A with the SEC. This form is called a contested proxy solicitation and it usually contains a letter to shareholders presenting the case for why shareholders should align themselves with the activists.

Form DEFC 14A should not be confused with Form DEF 14A, which is a definitive proxy statement that must be filed by or on behalf of a registrant when a shareholder vote is required. Companies file Form DEF 14A before every annual meeting to enable shareholders to vote by proxy.

By searching SEC's EDGAR database for filings of Form DEFC 14A, you can find undervalued companies that can eventually be properly valued if activist investors succeed in making changes.

# Schedule TO-I – Tender Offers

When companies buy back their shares, they can do it in the open market or through tender offers. In the open market, they buy shares just like everyone else. Through tender offers, they make an offer to buy a certain number of shares at a set price. This way, they can purchase a significant number of shares without moving the stock price.

To find tender offers, search SEC's EDGAR for filings of Schedule TO-I. The companies have to file this form with the SEC to announce tender offers.

Tender offer investing is a special situation investing method that can generate small returns in short periods of time. For example, if a company announces a tender offer to purchase shares for $11 per share, the traders will cause the stock price to trade below that number because there are some risks associated with the tender offer going through. So, the stock can trade at about $10 per share with a tender offer on the table at $11 per share.

As a tender investor, you can purchase the stock for $10 per share and sell it/tender it to the company for $11 per share, making a quick profit of $1 per share in the process.

# Schedule 13E-3 – Going Private

Companies go public for various reasons such as to gain access to capital markets or to make their shares liquid. However, sometimes being public carries more costs than benefits. Consequently, some choose to go private.

The going private transaction can happen when an outside firm (private equity firm) or the management offers to buy all the shares from existing shareholders. They usually offer some kind of premium over the trading price.

For example, if the stock is trading for $9.50 per share, they might offer shareholders $11 per share to sell. After the deal is announced, the stock price will trade at a slight discount to the offer price.

As an investor, you can purchase the stock and sell it to the management or the private equity firm at a slight profit when the going private transaction closes. Like tender offer transactions, going private transactions are a type of special situation investing. One way to find these deals is to search for Schedule 13E-3 filings.

# Form 425 – Mergers

erger arbitrage is also a type of special situations investing. The opportunity presents itself when another company offers to buy shares of a target company at a premium to incentivize investors to sell.

Like tender offers and going private transactions, you buy the shares of the target company after the announcement in the hope that you will be able to resell them to the acquirer at the pre-determined price/closing price, which is higher than what you paid. The key to analyzing merger deals is to determine the probability of the deal closing.

To find merger announcements, search SEC's EDGAR for filings of Form 425.

Another way to generate merger investment opportunities is by visiting Mergerinvesting.com. The site lists pending mergers with the closing price and last trading price showing you the spread that you can make.

# Overlooked Markets and Exchanges

When people hear the word "stock exchange" they automatically think of the New York Stock Exchange or the NASDAQ. While these two exchanges are the most prestigious places to list stocks, they are not the only ones. There are stock exchanges all over the world.

After the passage of the Sarbanes-Oxley Act in 2002, it became more expensive to be listed on US exchanges. Other exchanges like the AIM in London have capitalized on it by attracting companies looking for stock exchanges with fewer regulatory burdens.

While more and more public companies are choosing to use non-US exchanges to float their shares, most investors are still stuck in the past. They pretty much ignore and overlook investment opportunities on other exchanges.

You should consider looking at other exchanges like the AIM or TSX Venture Exchange because they list some very good companies. At the end of the day, it does not matter where the company is listed. What matters is that they have a good business that is profitable and will continue to grow. The stock price will take care of itself. If you find them on overlooked exchanges, you have a better chance of buying them at decent prices.

# Future Uplisting

M any companies that trade on lower-level exchanges or marketplaces want to eventually uplist to more prestigious exchanges. For example, some companies trading on the OTC Markets want to eventually trade on the NASDAQ or NYSE.

From an investor's point of view, it can be profitable to buy stocks of such companies before they uplist and watch the stock price increase after more investors are allowed to buy the stock on a higher-level exchange.

To find future uplisters, you have to be like a detective looking for clues in the press releases and news feeds. Companies that want to uplist must satisfy financial, corporate governance, and share price requirements. For example, the NASDAQ requires a share price of $4 per share.

Consequently, companies prepare in advance. They appoint independent directors to satisfy corporate governance requirements and they do a reverse split to satisfy share price requirements. As a detective investor, you want to search for press releases and news announcements that mention the appointment of independent directors and reverse stock splits.

For a list of stock splits and reverse stock splits, visit: Otcmarkets.com/market-activity/splits.

# Uplisted Companies

While on many occasions the stock price will jump when the company uplists to a higher exchange, the runway for future appreciation may be far from over. Many companies uplist because their businesses are doing well and will continue doing well in the future. So, if you buy them when they uplist and hold them long term, you may generate decent returns.

In the previous section, you had to be a detective to find future uplisters. Here you do not have to work so hard because the uplisting has already taken place.

Visit the following link to get a list of venue changes.

Otcmarkets.com/market-activity/venue-changes

Note that this list includes all venue changes meaning uplisting and delisting.

# Delisted Companies

Whe companies cannot maintain an exchange's listing requirements, they can get delisted. In the US, they get delisted to over-the-counter markets. The majority of the time, they get thrown out from the exchanges for very good reasons. Consequently, they usually continue to decline and you should not consider investing in them.

However, there are two types of delistings: voluntary and involuntary. When they are forced out, the delisting is involuntary. When they choose to delist, they do so voluntarily. These are the kinds of delistings that you should investigate. Find out why they are delisting. Is the company going private? It is being acquired?

Whether the delisting is voluntary or involuntary, investors tend to sell it off no matter what. Some institutional investors cannot own the stocks of delisted companies so they will sell regardless of value.

To find a list of delisters, visit the same source as in the previous section.

Otcmarkets.com/market-activity/venue-changes

# Index Additions

Money managers live and die based on how well their performance compares to various indexes such as the S&P 500, Dow, or Russell 2000. Because they may lose their jobs if they underperform in comparison to a particular index, they tend invest in stocks that are included in that index.

Consequently, when particular stocks are added to an index, there is automatic demand for their shares causing the stock price to increase in the short term.

Some investors specialize in figuring out which companies are going to be added to the index and buying them before it happens. If you want to follow such an event-driven strategy, the biggest index-rebalancing opportunity is the Russell Index reconstitution.

Every June, the Russell Indexes are rebalanced. However, before the final rebalancing is announced, there is a series of preannouncements. First, the preliminary additions and deletions are revealed. Then, they are revised a couple of times. At the end, the final list of published.

As an investor, you can buy some stocks from the preliminary list before the additions are finalized.

To get the list, visit the following link and choose among the additions or deletions listed for the various indexes.

Ftserussell.com/research-insights/russell-reconstitution

# Index Deletions

When companies are deleted from indexes, they may be sold off beyond what is justifiable based on the underlying fundamentals. The reason why they were deleted could have been a temporary decrease in their market capitalization, which caused them to fall outside of the index's criteria. Money managers who hold hundreds of stocks in their portfolios often dump recently deleted stocks simply because they are no longer part of the index, and they do not investigate the reasons behind why they were deleted.

As an investor, it is your job to study them and figure out whether their businesses are permanently damaged or whether they will bounce back and eventually be added back to the index they were deleted from. Any time there is selling unrelated to the performance of the business, it can create an opportunity for you, but you have to do your homework. To find index deletions, search for indexes that interest you.

# Hated Indexes

Companies are categorized into indexes to show the price performance of various groups. Indexes can be based on a country, region, exchange, market capitalization, or industry. For example, the S&P 500 is country specific while the NASDAQ 100 is exchange specific.

There are times when specific groups fall out of favor. For example, specific countries, industries, and regions can be hated for one reason or another. So, if you want to invest in a hated group, you can simply find an index that represents that group.

For example, beginning in 2011, the entire gold and silver mining sector declined significantly. GDX and GDXJ are indexes that represent major and junior miners, respectively. If you believe that an entire sector is a good place to invest, you can either buy the entire index that represents it or dig inside to select the best companies within that index.

To figure out what is hated, look at the price performance of specific indexes or read the financial news.

### Vanguard Index Performance

- Personal.vanguard.com/us/funds/tools/benchmarkreturns

### Morningstar Index Performance

- News.morningstar.com/index/indexreturn.html

### Barchart Index Performance

- Barchart.com/stocks/indices.php

# Company Name Changes

I t is not unusual for companies to change their names. They may do so for various reasons. Sometimes the name change can lead to positive outcomes in the future and sometimes the name change has no effect at all.

When a young and growing company changes its name, it is usually because it wants to expand its product offering and/or geographical coverage. This is fantastic because such a change may lead to increases in revenues and profits. As an investor, you definitely want to keep an eye on such companies.

However, when an old and established company changes its name, it might mean that it wants to put its bad past behind it. If the only thing that changes is the name, then you want to stay away from companies like this because the past will simply become the future.

For a list of company name changes, follow this link:

Otcmarkets.com/market-activity/company-name-changes

You can find a list of company name changes along with ticker symbol changes at this link:

Otcmarkets.com/market-activity/symbol-name-changes

---

# Company News

As you know, publicly traded companies have to keep their investors updated on the developments of their businesses. Some information releases are more important than others. Because the SEC requires companies to file particular forms associated with certain actions, it is possible to find companies by searching for those forms.

However, some developments do not require any forms. For example, when a company introduces a new product or adds a new client, it does not have to file any forms with the SEC. If the event is material, it will disclose it through news or press releases. So, we need a way to search for news or find news feeds for publicly traded companies.

Google News is great when you know what you are searching for. Type in "buybacks," "activist investor," or "tender offer" and you will likely get a list of candidates to analyze.

If you want to obtain news feeds for companies on particular exchanges or industries, you will need to pay Factset or Bloomberg to provide you with that data.

However, if you focus on companies trading on the OTC Markets, you can get their news data for free:

- Otcmarkets.com/news/otc-news
- Otcmarkets.com/news/otc-market-headlines

# Keyword Search

The reason why it is time consuming to find investment ideas is because you have to familiarize yourself with the thesis. In other words, you have to do a lot of reading. Many times, you have to dig inside the various filings, such as the 10-Ks and 10-Qs, to get the story.

If you know what kind of opportunities you are looking for, you can use certain keywords to search through all the SEC filings similar to how Google searches the Internet. For example, you can search for discontinued operations, product introductions, and tender offers.

10kwizard.com is a commercial service owned by Morningstar that allows you to search the SEC filings of publicly traded companies. You can search by many different criteria including a keyword search. It is one of the best tools available for this type of search. The professional version of 10kwizard costs $802 per month. However, Morningstar will be discontinuing the service at the end of August 2016 and transitioning subscribers to Intelligize.com, a similar website.

# SEC Info

As you know, the SEC operates EDGAR, which is a database of SEC filings. While EDGAR contains a wealth of information, it is not the most user friendly. It has gotten better over the years, but it can be frustrating. Consequently, various entrepreneurs have created websites and services that take data from EDGAR and present it in more readable formats.

SEC Info (Secinfo.com) is a website designed by a former investment banker. It is a fantastic website for investors who want to search by the type of form. You can find tender offers, insider buys, late filing notices, bankruptcy filings, and much more. The site is free for most users.

# Capital IQ

Capital IQ, Factset, and Bloomberg Professional Service are powerful research tools. They each cost more than $10,000 per year and offer various subscription models.

Capital IQ is a division of Standard & Poor's. It was founded in 1998. It provides research, screening, real-time market data, backtesting, portfolio management, financial modeling, and quantitative analysis. Its coverage includes more than two million public and private companies world-wide.

All the information provided by Capital IQ is public, and anyone can get it themselves through their own research. However, thousands of investment managers, hedge funds, private equity firms, and advisory firms use the service because it makes their lives easier. They can quickly access large amounts of data all in one place, saving them time and money. For example, they can download several years' worth of financial data into a Microsoft Excel spreadsheet with the click of a mouse.

In order to justify the cost of Capital IQ, you probably need to have a significant amount of money under management. However, if you are unable to afford a subscription to Capital IQ, you might want to try the library of a local university, which may subscribe to it.

# FactSet

FactSet is a software platform for investment research. It provides access to data that is similar to what Capital IQ provides, but it is more expensive. FactSet is owned by FactSet Research Systems, which is a publicly traded company whose stock trades on the NYSE under the ticker symbol FDS.

FactSet has a much longer history than Capital IQ. It was founded in 1978, so it is 20 years older than Capital IQ. It provides real-time news and quotes, company and portfolio analysis, multi-company comparison, industry analysis, company screening, portfolio optimization and simulation, predictive risk measurements, alpha testing, and tools to value companies.

For professionals who can afford subscriptions, FactSet definitely proves valuable because the client retention rate is more than 90 percent. Some investment professionals subscribe to both Capital IQ and FactSet.

# Bloomberg

Bloomberg Professional Service is still referred to as Bloomberg Terminal by financial professionals because historically, clients received a physical terminal through which they accessed the service. It is a service provided by Bloomberg L.P., a company founded by former New York City Mayor Michael Bloomberg in 1981.

Bloomberg Professional Service is an investment research service that is very popular among financial professionals. It costs $24,000 per year. While it also provides certain features such as screening tools and financial analysis tools, it excels in providing real-time data, news, and analytics for markets all over the world. It does so for all the asset classes such as commodities, derivatives, equities, fixed income, and foreign exchange.

With this information, you know what is going on in all the markets at all times. By using this macro data, you can find markets that are hated and oversold very quickly. Then, you can research individual companies based on that.

Bloomberg Professional Service also offers research from sell-side and independent research firms, using more than 1,500 sources. This is also very useful when conducting due diligence.

# OSV Stock Analysis Software

Capital IQ, FactSet, and Bloomberg Professional Service are fantastic tools for analyzing and finding investment ideas, but they are expensive. If you are a small investor, you most likely will not be able to afford their prices.

Jae Jun of Old School Value (Oldschoolvalue.com) developed a stock analysis software program that can perform some of the same functions as these expensive services at a fraction of the cost ($399 per year).

Old School Value Stock Analysis Software allows you to enter a ticker symbol for US-listed stocks to generate several pages of analytical data. The software downloads financial statements for the past 10 years and the last several quarters. It also calculates various financial and valuation ratios.

By using this program, you can quickly sort through many companies to eliminate unwanted candidates and focus on studying only companies that look promising. This is a huge timesaver. What the software can do for you in seconds would take you days or weeks to do manually.

# Value Line
# Investment Survey

Value Line (Valueline.com) is an independent research firm that provides comprehensive research on thousands of stocks. The company was founded by Arnold Bernhard in 1931 after he saw his mother lose all of her savings during the 1929 stock market crash. He developed a system that would measure and signal when stocks were overvalued and undervalued.

Because of its long history, some of the most renowned investors, such as Warren Buffet and Peter Lynch, have used it in their research.

Value Line publishes one-page stock reports for the individual companies that it covers. Each report gives you a quick glance into the business because it contains current and historical financial data, financial results, three- to five-year price and earnings projections, price charts, a ranking, and a short written analysis. The company also provides various screens to help investors narrow down their investment ideas.

Subscriptions cost between $116 and $795 per year depending on the type of service. Many local libraries have access to Value Line Investment Survey.

# Old Recommendations

Some of my best investment ideas have come from old recommendations of stocks that other investors have abandoned. When investors or newsletter writers recommend an idea on Value Investors Club or SumZero, they present their investment thesis. A lot of times, the thesis takes longer to play out than expected or the thesis does not play out in the way that it was supposed to and investors throw in the towel.

Look through old ideas that have declined 50, 60, or 80 percent from the time that they were recommended and analyze whether they are still good investment opportunities. Very few people do this because they only read about new and exciting ideas.

When you look through ideas that have disappointed and exhausted investors, you face very little competition. You can contact the original writer for an update. More often than not, the person still follows the story and can update you very quickly.

Call the CEO and ask what has happened with the company since the recommendation was written. The thesis might still be the same but if the stock price is lower, you will get a better return because your entry price is lower.

# Trends

I am sure you have heard the expression that the trend is your friend. Well, this is because it is true. There are powerful trends all around us and if you can identify them, they can lead you to profitable investment ideas.

For example, ten years ago, you barely heard anything about organic foods. Now, it is part of our everyday vocabulary. Every time you enter a grocery store, you see an organic foods section. There were people who identified this trend early on and benefited from it by investing in companies such as Whole Foods. You can do the same with future trends.

Go to Amazon and search for books about future trends. Search the Internet for articles on trends. There are hundreds of them. Yes, some of the trends are dumb and you cannot make money on them but there are many that can make you rich.

Once you identify a trend, figure out which companies will benefit from it. This is the hard part because many times the early entrants are not the ones that reap the benefits.

Sometimes the latecomers learn from their predecessors' mistakes and enter the market better equipped.

# Problems

New products and services are born out of problems and frustration. Figure out where problems exist and find out which companies are working on products to solve them. In the past, Wall Street's sell side controlled all the information about publicly traded companies. This was creating a huge problem for the buy side. They did not trust Wall Street to provide them with unbiased information on the financial products that they were selling.

To solve the information problem for the buy side, Michael Bloomberg founded Bloomberg Terminal, and before that, Arnold Bernhard founded Value Line Investment Survey. These two companies made their founders and shareholders extremely wealthy.

Look around. What kind of problems do we have?

- Smartphones are constantly distracting us.
- Smartphone batteries have a short battery life.
- Many schools are doing a poor job of educating students.
- The nation's transportation infrastructure is deteriorating.
- We still do not have a cure for cancer.

You get the idea. There are millions of problems that need to be solved. Identify them, no matter how small, and they will lead you to investment opportunities.

# Companies with New Products

Companies are in the business of satisfying their customers by providing products and services. The moment they stop satisfying their customers, they lose them. This is why they constantly have to develop new products and improve existing ones.

New products that successfully satisfy customers will generate future revenues. However, when you wait for revenues to show up in the financial statements, most of the gains have already been made because screens are very good at performing quantitative searches.

Consequently, when scanning news from publicly traded companies (through Google News, FactSet, or Bloomberg), pay attention to new product launches. Study the companies with new products. Determine what problems the new products solve. Talk to customers to hear their side of the story. Determine the size of the market. Invest if the future revenue and profits are not priced into the stock.

# New Product Halo Effect

Have you ever seen a new product and said to yourself "Darn, I wish I had thought of that." We all have. However, I bet you never ask yourself what kinds of other products will be developed as a result of this new product.

When a new product is developed, it solves a particular problem, but then it creates several other problems. For example, when Apple came out with a smartphone, plenty of other problems and demands were created and someone benefited from solving them.

Some new products that were developed as a result of the smartphone are phone cases, mobile backup batteries, camera lens mounts, and game controllers.

ZAGG, a screen shield company, was a huge home run for investors who were smart enough to buy the stock at the beginning. However, without the invention of the smartphone, ZAGG would have never created such a successful product.

Be on the lookout for the introduction of new products. Study them and figure out what new problems they create.

Ask customers what they like and don't like about them. Ask them what they would fix and read reviews online. Then, find companies that are working on halo products to address the new problems. You will face very little competition from other investors who are glued to their Bloomberg terminals crunching the numbers.

# Legislation Beneficiaries

E very day, lawmakers are working on new laws to be passed for all sorts of reasons. Abortion, same-sex marriage, and the legalization of marijuana are only some of the topics debated by lawmakers. There are thousands of other issues discussed that never even make the news.

When a law changes, opportunities are created. Who will be the winners and losers? Who will have to pay more to satisfy the new requirements? Who will provide the products and services to satisfy the new requirements? Will there be new products or services developed to comply with the law? If so, who will develop them?

The following are two sites that you can use to track changes in legislation.

- GovTrack – Govtrack.us
- Open Congress – Opencongress.org

On GovTrack you can search bills by status or by subject area, such as agriculture, education, or health. The Open Congress website allows you to search by lawmaker's name, issue area, or bill number.

# Hiring Companies

Companies that are struggling lay off employees and companies that are growing hire employees. So, by finding companies that are hiring, you might find decent investment opportunities.

There are many way to generate a list of businesses that are hiring. You can look for them the same way employees look for jobs on sites such as

- Indeed.com
- Linkup.com
- Simplyhired.com

You can also read various articles on the Internet featuring businesses that are hiring. For example, Forbes published an article titled "10 Hot Companies That Are Hiring Like Crazy." One of the companies listed was Morningstar, which is a stock I used to own.

When you find public companies that are hiring, do not automatically assume that the company is profitable. It may simply have high employee turnover, or it might have just raised money by selling stock and is now on a spending spree. The healthiest companies pay for new hires with internally generated cash flows.

# Division Sellers

When you are looking at a company's financial statements, you are looking at the financial performance of consolidated businesses. This means that the individual financial performances of all of the business units are combined together. However, not all business units are of the same quality. Some are more profitable than others.

It is not unusual for a company with several business segments to have one that is performing so poorly that it makes the overall performance of the company look bad. As a result, investors give up and drive down the stock price.

To improve its financial performance, the company may sell the underperforming division. If you can identify such companies before the consolidated financial statements improve as a result of such a sale, you can generate positive investment returns. To find such companies, you can scan headlines for division sales or search 10kwizard.com for phrases such as "discontinued operations."

When you compile a list of companies that have sold business divisions, you need to figure out why they sold them. There is always a reason.

# Strategic Alternatives

W hen the management or shareholders are not happy with the valuation the market is assigning the stock, they might look into strategic alternatives to rectify the mispricing. Strategic alternatives could mean several things such as selling the entire company, selling a division, merging with another company, or acquiring another company.

When a company makes an announcement about strategic alternatives, a possible investment opportunity presents itself. You need to investigate what this is all about. Why is the company doing it? What is it trying to accomplish? Was the management forced to take this route by major or activist investors? What are the likely outcomes from strategic alternatives? Is there money to be made?

To generate a list of companies exploring strategic alternatives, you can scan companies' news and/or keyword search Google News and 10kwizard.

# Management Changes

M anagement changes happen for all sorts of reasons. Members of the management team retire, find different jobs, are fired, or leave for health reasons. Unfortunately, as a public shareholder, you rarely know the true reason behind management departures. They are carefully planned and explained so as to not cause any panic.

However, most of the time, the truth is that someone is unhappy with the status quo. Either shareholders and directors are unhappy with the management or the management is unhappy with the business and/or shareholders and directors.

Whatever the case may be, big changes might be coming and you need to find out what is going on. What forced the management out? Is there a new shareholder that was accumulating shares (look for 13D and 13G filings)? Was the stock price declining? Are there new directors? Did anyone start a proxy fight? Who are the new managers? Who brought them on?

By searching for companies with management changes, you can find investment opportunities that are in the process of major transformations which can turn out to be extremely profitable. Again, you will find these opportunities by searching the news and performing keyword searches on investment research websites.

# Board of Directors Changes

T he board of directors is a group of individuals whose purpose is to represent shareholders. Without the board of directors, the shareholders would be at the mercy of the management. When the composition of the board changes, something is up.

The board members might be dissatisfied with the way the management is operating the company. They may want to leave before bad things happen. Shareholders might be dissatisfied with the board members for being "yes men" to the management. The management might be dissatisfied with the board members for micromanaging.

Search and pay attention to companies whose board members resign and are replaced with new ones. If it happens more than once in a short period of time, then something major might be taking place within the company. You have to put your investigative hat on and go to work.

# Major Client Additions

Companies constantly add and lose clients in the course of business. They do not announce it to the world every time it happens because it is not material. However, when a company gets a major client, it has to announce it to the market. Sometimes, in the press release, it will disclose the monetary business potential from the new client.

By scanning through the headlines of companies' press releases, you can find businesses whose revenues are about to explode. It is not unusual for investors to completely ignore the news because client additions do not immediately add to the bottom line especially when the client is testing the company with a small order.

Sevcon, a manufacturer of AC and DC motor controllers, is a perfect example. The company developed an improved product and started signing up clients. In the press releases, it kept announcing new agreements with major clients. The market was ignoring them. Then, all of a sudden it mattered because the revenues began to grow. The stock price increased from $3 to $12 in a short period of time even though investors could have seen the signs of improvements by reading the press releases.

# Major Client Losses

Investors are funny creatures. They may ignore new client additions for a long time, but when it comes to major client losses, they do not forget how to press the sell button. They can go so far overboard with heavy selling that after such an announcement, the company's market capitalization can decline far beyond anything reasonable.

For example, Marchex is a company with two businesses. One is an advertising business and the other one is just a portfolio of websites. In 2014, the company lost a major client and the stock price declined from $12 per share to $3.50 per share in a short period of time. The sell-off was considerably overdone. The market capitalization of the company declined so much that it ended up being less than the value of the website portfolio (the second business). This meant that you were getting the advertising business for free.

Obviously, sometimes when a company loses a major client, the decrease in the stock price is justifiable, but the loss in itself might be your opportunity. When you find companies in such situations, look to see if they have other business segments. Estimate what this loss will mean to the value of the company. Figure out why the client left because it might mean that more client losses will follow.

# Disaster Victims

D isasters can ruin lives, cities, and businesses. However, they can make you a lot of money because investors tend to overact to them.

In April 2010, oil and gas company BP experienced a deepwater oil spill from its Macondo well. The spill was all over the news and BP's stock price was cut in half within days of the spill. Yes, the accident was a total disaster but investors overacted. BP was not going to go out of business. The demand for oil and gas was not going anywhere. The company was generating free cash flow from other projects unrelated to the Macondo well. Because of the overreaction, the stock price almost doubled when the spill was contained and investors came to their senses.

There are plenty of potentially profitable opportunities to buy stock in disaster victim companies. Sometimes entire industries are affected. Think of 9/11 and how it affected the entire airline industry.

Next time something bad happens, make a list of companies whose stock was hurt by it and investigate whether investors went too far with the selling. Estimate the worst case scenario of what can happen to the company's revenues. Find out if the company owns more than one business segment because if the disaster destroyed one business, the other one might be perfectly fine and you might be able to buy it for pennies on the dollar.

# Investigation Victims

Shareholders of public companies hate issues. Most only want to own companies that are performing well and experiencing no major problems. The one thing that they fear the most are investigations of a company, especially federal investigations.

Investigations create so much uncertainty, stoking investors' fear to the point that they will sell the stock at any price and creating a buying opportunity for you.

As of the date of this book, Lumber Liquidators is being investigated for selling floors that can cause cancer. The stock price declined from $70 to $20 per share as a result of negative publicity. Some investors are using the investigation as an opportunity to buy shares.

To find companies that are being investigated, just open a newspaper or read articles on the Internet. Of course, you can also scan companies' press releases for announcements of an investigation.

When you find candidates to research, study the situation. Why is the company being investigated? What will be the penalty for being found guilty? It a settlement likely?

Could the entire business be shut down? Does the company own any other businesses that are unrelated to the investigation? Does the company have enough cash to pay for the penalty?

# Dividend Cutters

nvestors own stocks for two reasons: capital appreciation and dividends. Companies that are growing fast usually do not pay dividends because they reinvest everything back into the business. Companies that are mature or that are in certain industries, such as REITs or utility stocks, pay dividends on a regular basis. Consequently, they attract an investor base, such as retired people, that relies on dividend income.

When companies cut a dividend, then dividend-dependent investors no longer have a reason to own the stock. So, they sell it. If enough of them sell it, the stock price might go down below the underlying value. This is a perfect opportunity for long-term investors.

You have to learn why the dividend was cut and the probability of it being reinstated in the future. You still need to like the business. Don't buy it just because it stopped paying dividends. The company might be in trouble and may have chosen to cut the dividend to slow down its eventual death.

**Stocks that cut dividends:**

- Tradingstockalerts.com/PremiumAlerts/DividendCutters

**Companies in risk of cutting dividends:**

- Dividenddetective.com/dividend_death_list.htm

# Activist Insight

Activist Insight (Activistinsight.com) is a research company dedicated to the activist investing space. It is headquartered in London and provides two products: Activist Insight Online (contact the company for individual pricing plans) and Activism Monthly Premium magazine ($495 per year).

Activist Insight Online provides profiles of more than 500 activist investors worldwide. It also keeps subscribers up to date with all the activist situations around the world. The product is updated daily.

Activist Monthly Premium magazine is similar to Value Investor Insight newsletter, but it focuses on activist investing. It includes interviews with key players, the latest activist campaigns, and critical developments in the field of activist investing.

If you like investment opportunities where activist investors are pushing for changes, then Activist Insight can help you. The firm also provides free reports where you can learn about activist investing and be exposed to investment opportunities.

# Post-Bankruptcy Companies

Bankruptcy is the worst thing that common shareholders can experience because it usually means that the value of their shares is wiped out. However, sophisticated investors can benefit from investing in post-bankruptcy companies because so many investors are not familiar with the process.

When companies are pushed into bankruptcy, they can either declare Chapter 7 or Chapter 11 bankruptcy. With Chapter 7, the company stops all operations and goes completely out of business. The assets are sold to pay off debt. With Chapter 11, the company continues to operate and the capital structure is reorganized. Public companies prefer the Chapter 11 route when possible.

During reorganization, brand-new shares are issued and distributed to stakeholders in the following order: secured creditors, unsecured creditors, and common shareholders. So, at the end of the day, the creditors become the new common shareholders and the company becomes debt free.

The new shares are floated on the market but they are in the hands of stakeholders who have had a bad experience with the company. Also, they might be debt investors who happened to inherit common shares in the bankruptcy reorganization. When they have an opportunity to sell, they frequently do. But the problem is that there are not very many buyers because the new shares were not promoted through road shows or any other type of promotions. They may send the new stock price so low that it makes sense for you to buy shares from them assuming the company is now healthy with no debt burden.

# Companies in Bankruptcy

When people say that you should not invest in bankrupt companies, they are almost right. You should not invest in the common shares of companies in bankruptcy. However, from the previous section you learned that after a Chapter 11 bankruptcy reorganization, new shares will be issued first to all the creditors and then, if any value is left, to common shareholders.

You can acquire the new shares in two ways. One way is to buy them after they start trading in the secondary market. The second way is to buy them by acquiring the debt from creditors. Then, when the new shares are issued, they will be issued to you because you are now the creditor.

Investing in bankruptcies and post-bankruptcies can be very lucrative but it is more complicated than investing in healthy companies. Consequently, before you jump in with both feet, I suggest you educate yourself on the subject. Read *Distress Investing* by Martin J. Whitman.

# Become an Analyst

As you can see, there are lots of ways to find investment opportunities in a world where there are thousands of publicly traded companies. It is simply not possible to use them all. You would have to stop eating and sleeping and you would still not be able to use them all.

The good news is that you do not have to know about thousands of companies. All you need are a few winners and you can accomplish your investment goals. To find several stocks that will deliver great returns, make a list of 30, 50, or 100 companies and become their analyst.

Follow them, read their reports, study their products, and get to know their management. It is better if you chose companies that are not widely followed so that you can get an informational edge. You will be amazed how well you can do by keeping a close eye on these companies.

If you talk to the management or investor relations department of each company once a month, you will know exactly when it is the best time to invest in them and when it is better to stay away. I have a list of about 20 companies that I follow very closely and I know more about them than anybody else simply because I keep them fresh in my mind.

# Turning Over Rocks

W e all wish that we could just simply go to a place or website and be handed great investment opportunities. This is why we look for shortcuts—newsletters, screeners, or forms filed with the SEC. This is understandable because we are all extremely busy.

However, if you want to be the best of the best, you have to find your own investment ideas and turn over lots of rocks as Warren Buffett used to say. This means studying one company after another. Like this, you will find opportunities that are not on anybody's radar. They are way off the map. Yes, this is hard work, but the experience that you will get from it is priceless.

If you looked at 10 companies per day, over the course of one year you would have looked at 3,650 ideas. This means that you could know all the companies trading on the NASDAQ. How many investors have done that?

If you went through such an exercise, you would not need to pay anyone for investment ideas because you would find more deals than you could handle. Also, imagine how much you would learn in the process. In one year, you would learn more about investing than any MBA student or analyst at a hedge fund.

Made in the USA
Monee, IL
28 May 2020

32096210R00095